Kickin' Eighty
Nibbling at Ninety

Pat Hurlbut Sellars

DEDICATION

I dedicate this book to my parents,
Mary and David Hurlbut, Sr. whose
courage brought me into this world
in the face of great adversity.

CONTENTS

ACKNOWLEDGMENTS

A special thanks to my dear author friend, Annemarie Eveland, for her encouragement and countless hours of work to get my book completed.

Thank you to my three daughters Shari, Deborah and Karen and their families for their generosity and support.

And Connie Cockrell, for her assistance with final editing and formatting.

Introduction

*T*oday is Monday, March 1, 2021 and I am writing my first book entitled *Kickin' Eighty* (Nibbling at Ninety.) I am eighty-eight years old. It is my birthday and as I was told from childhood, "Age is just a number." I agree as I am still here!

My Mom was in her forties when she became pregnant with me. My parents had four living children in grammar school and high school. They lost a baby eight years before and were assured that there would be no more children.

When my mom went to her doctor and declared that she was pregnant, he smiled and said, "It is a tumor, Mary, to which she replied, "It is a very lively one!" I did not like being called a tumor, so I kicked.

The doctor then went on to say that on the slim chance if I lived, I would most likely be mentally impaired. There was an option. My dad and mom both said, boy or girl, it will be fine!!!

I was born in Milford hospital in Milford, Connecticut on March 1, 1933, during the Depression. I was a 6 ½ pound beauty (my words.) I had long black hair and a very loud voice, (and I still do!).

From the outset, I have been extremely healthy. I take no medications, only an important array of vitamins. My hair is flirting with gray. I exercise in bed before I get up in the morning and walk, at least, thirty minutes daily. I stretch frequently during the day.

The Depression days were rough, especially when a new baby is on the way. We did not have a great deal of money. My dad worked when he could find a job. He was known to give money for gas to my brothers who had work, and he hitch hiked himself.

However, we never seemed to go without. We had a modest home, albeit one bathroom. Did anyone have more at the time? My mom's mantra was – "You spend money, first, on necessities;" and food was number one. "Eat Right and Stay Well!" We always had an abundance of food and always organic!

Sometimes, people would pay my dad with food. One time someone gave him a goose. Now, I know what you are thinking – that goose was my constant companion and protector when I was a small child. I loved that goose, and it paved the way for my love for <u>all</u> critters in the future.

Looking back now, I realize how difficult it must have been to raise a baby at that time. However, I never once felt deprived, or unwanted or unloved.

Someone asked my parents if they were going to have a "little Mike" to go along with Pat. My mom's reply to the sarcasm was, "We take them as they come!" A few years later, under very different circumstances, it did happen.

Why am I writing this book now you may ask? Partly because I love to write, and I have since I was a small child. Partly, because it is time to look back on my own life.

Even with my years of experience, I can still learn something. Just possibly, I can give, in a small way, some insight to those who face the challenge of "living."

My quick advice is "Never Give Up!" "Never Grow Up!" (I still feel like a child at heart.) "Never lose your sense of humor!" "Always look for that small, buried nugget that comes with, not only good experiences, but especially, with the <u>bad</u> <u>ones</u>!"

CHAPTER 1
THE YOUNGER YEARS

I feel very fortunate that I was born into an educated family. My dad's father, Joseph Hurlbut, was a graduate of the Hartt School of music in Hartford, Connecticut. My mom's dad, Nelson Edwards, graduated Phi Beta Kappa, from Wesleyan University in Middletown, Connecticut. He became a Methodist Minister. My mom's mother, Mary McLean, attended either Barnard College or Hunter College, in New York City. I do not know if she graduated.

In no way am I bragging. I feel

that this was unusual in the 1800s. On down the line, education has always been stressed.

When I was born, I had two brothers and two sisters – Nel, 17, Rena, 15, David, 13 and Merle 11.

At around the age of three, my brothers delighted in teaching me how to read. I knew the word "ESSO" very well. They were grooming me to marry a Rockefeller, (perhaps?)

In 1938, we had the worst hurricane to date. Our home on Atwater Street, in Point Beach, Connecticut, was about two city blocks from Long Island Sound. The water came up to our house.

My dad and my two brothers spent all night rescuing people. They borrowed row boats to make the rescues. Some people did not want to leave and that caused a hassle. One woman would not leave her parrot, so they had to go back for it.

My mom and I were evacuated to the Merwins. They had a beautiful house on the hill. It was across New

Haven Avenue and not far from our home. How gracious they were to take us in.

They had two daughters. I believe their names were Marie and Eunice. I think Eunice is the one who taught me how to ride a bike.

The devastation from the hurricane was so unbelievable. I remember seeing a grand piano and other valuable items floating in the Sound. The loss of life was heartbreaking.

~ ~ ~

At the age of five or six, or earlier, I began piano lessons and dancing lessons. I became smitten with ballet.

I started my VISION LIST at this time. "Vision" meaning in this case, seeing and imagining the future "Numero Uno" "Famous Ballet Dancer." I began writing, (mostly poetry.) The title of this book, "Kickin' 80" was inspired by my short career as a dancer.

In the first grade, I studied about Egypt. I was fascinated by the pictures and the stories. Travel immediately took "top spot" on my VISION LIST and has remained there, ever since. GOALS are a big priority in my life!

The first trip that I remember was by car to Washington D.C. It was a visit to my mom's sister, my Aunt Ethel and her husband, Ed. They had a thriving real estate business in D.C. and the surrounding area.

The next time we visited, was at Easter. My uncle arranged for me to go to the White House for the Easter Egg Roll, I believe they called it. President Roosevelt, Eleanor and three or four of their children were present.

This time, we took an extensive tour of the city, which my parents felt was very important <u>for me</u>.

Fluffy, their dog, stayed home to guard the apartment. She got hungry and ate the contents of my beautiful Easter basket. She lived, but I could have killed her. It was totally my fault. I had been warned!

Holidays were always very special in our home, and I remember Christmas very well that year.

I was attending Central Grammar School, which was close to the center of Milford, where my brother, Nel, worked. He would drive me home. Each day, I would visit a local store to look at a beautiful doll on display. I knew my parents could not afford her, but it was fun dreaming, anyway.

Every Christmas eve, my dad would read Christmas Stories from a special book. (How I wish we had kept it.) He always ended with "Twas the Night Before Christmas."

My mother would start baking her famous culinary desserts. Then, she and my dad would prepare the turkey, which cooked all night. My dad would bake his bread. Just thinking about those wonderful aromas brings back such fond memories.

When Christmas day arrived that

year. I opened my stocking and
Merle had put coal in it. I was
devastated. I knew I deserved it, but
nevertheless.

Sometimes I would answer the
phone, a "no-no." Merle was very
pretty and very popular. She had
many boyfriends. When one would
call and ask who she was out with, I
told them. Charming child, I was
truthful at least.

We always waited to open gifts
until Aunt Mabel and Uncle Cliff
arrived. Aunt Mabel's gifts were
always special because <u>she</u> made
them.

We usually received only one gift,
as money was tight. It never
bothered me because I learned early
that, "Money does not buy
happiness." Another <u>valuable</u>
lesson.

When I opened my gift, I was
stunned. It was "the doll." I never
even realized that they knew about
her! Believe it or not, I still have her.
Her shoes are gone and also her fur
cape. (I probably sold them.) But her

gown and slip, she still has. I also have a little brown bear; my brothers gave me. He looks like he's been through the war, but he sits proudly on my dresser.

I always looked forward to Memorial Day because we would get together with the relatives in the area. We would buy our poppies, in honor of those who died for our freedom. Then we would go to the Indian River Cemetery, in Clinton, Connecticut, to pay our respects to our loved ones buried there.

Afterwards, we would go to someone's house and spend the day visiting. Very emotional for me to remember, but again with very fond memories.

When I was seven, I took my first "solo" trip. My Uncle Ed had died, and my Aunt Ethel was living in Falls Church, Virginia, with her daughter Ethelwyn, and her new husband, John Meyer. They invited me to spend part of the summer with them on their farm. I was thrilled.

They had, at that time, what was called "Traveler's Aide." I left from New Haven, Connecticut by train, made a change and a nice employee helped me to find the correct connection to Washington, D.C. It all worked out fine. The family was waiting for me.

Uncle Ed's aunt, in her eighties, lived with them. When I met her, she was wearing the traditional long black dress and high button shoes. We spoke briefly, and then she picked up an axe and went outside to chop wood. Auntie Irene had been quite a "gal" in her day.

At breakfast, every morning, we would have interesting conversations. Auntie Irene would constantly repeat herself. I heard one story over and over about "Little Green Tomatoes." (It never bothered me.) I wish I could remember it today.

This was my first introduction to one of the many forms of dementia. Ironically, I would be working with people with this disease, as a C.N.A.

It would become very personal for me.

I loved every minute of that time spent on the farm in Virginia.

When I left, they gave me a baby duck to take home with me on the train.

The ride home was uneventful, until the duck got to "peeping." A lovely woman by the name of Flip Applebee, came to sit with me. She assured me that she would not let anyone take my duck. (Why I remember her name, to this day, is a mystery?)

The duck, of course, like my goose, was taken to a good home. I was never the wiser.

Back to school, I went, not realizing that this would be my last year living in Pt. Beach. I would be "starting over", so to speak in 1941.

CHAPTER 2
1941 - A YEAR TO REMEMBER

I remember this year so very
well. I loved my life in Point Beach,
Connecticut. I was doing very well at
Central Grammar School, in Milford.
I had a myriad of friends.

I was totally shaken when my
dad told me that we would be
moving to Woodmont, Connecticut.
It meant changing schools.

I had no idea he was even
contemplating this. When I
questioned him, he never gave me a
definitive answer, except, "I bought
a house, and we move mid-year."
WE DID!

For me, this change, was very difficult. I was very shy and really missed my old friends. The kids at the new school called me "stuck up" and other nasty names. I felt like a pariah.

When I spoke to my mother about it, she just said, "They are jealous." I guess that was the only excuse that came to her mind. She added, "Don't let them know it bothers you. Treat them nicely. Try harder."

My mother never cared what people said about her. She was very outspoken and very comfortable "in her own skin." I do not think that she could empathize with my feelings.

She did teach us all, good sound principles for living in this world. We went to church every Sunday. I would not have traded my early training for anything.

My sister, Rena, was now married to Ben Meyer. His father, John, was my cousin Ethelwyn's husband. My sister, Merle was dating Joe Boxwell and it looked like their marriage was imminent. She and Rena lived together in Boston.

My brothers were busy working, as was my dad, so I hardly ever saw them.

I would walk, or ride my bike down to the Sound. I would sit there for hours, because I was so <u>very</u> lonely.

In Point Beach, we always had a house full. Sundays were always the best. Because of my mom's culinary prowess, people would stop by, "just to say hello." In our house, you never left without something to eat or drink. But, NO ALCOHOL!!!

One bright spot – I would see my good friend, Ann Cornwall. We met when we were about four years old and lived on the same street in Point Beach.

We took dance classes together.

Ann was a beautiful tap dancer. Sometimes, I would play the piano when she did a solo. We performed in several shows that year. My dad, sometimes, did the lighting. I don't think we had the "Nutcracker" that December, however.

Her brothers were in high school with my siblings. Supposedly, our fathers were related through King Richard, the Lion Hearted. I'll have to check that out.

Ironically, when I moved to Green Valley, Arizona, years and years later, her brother and his wife lived close by. Howard and Pat became my good friends. Their daughter, Sherry Brown, is now my closest and dearest friend. I call her my "Fourth Daughter." Small, small world. I love her husband, Lloyd, and we consider ourselves family.

My dad kept up with politics and was very involved in New Haven, Connecticut. He and my Uncle Cliff, who lived in New Haven, spoke frequently and I would listen to their conversations.

At my age then, I did not understand all of the ramifications of those conversations.

My dad wanted me to learn and be aware of what was happening in the world. He would try to explain it, as simply as possible.

I knew that Germany had invaded Poland. One day we were talking about Hitler. I innocently commented that, "Hitler has done a lot of good for his people." (I heard that somewhere.) My dad said, "Hitler is not a good person, and he is not out to help his country, or its people. Hitler is out for himself." It proved to be <u>SO TRUE</u>.

President Roosevelt was not his favorite person. He questioned his policies and knew he was not well. Who would take his place, he wondered? He felt that the President could have definitely shortened the Depression. Now he was questioning why all our planes were grouped together in Hawaii?

As the year progressed, things became all the more volatile and our involvement in the war more and more likely. Germany was taking over Europe, piece by piece. Winston Churchill's name was very well known. (What they did to him later, was a disgrace!)

On Sunday, December 7, 1941, my mom and I went to church at Woodmont Chapel for the service. It was there that we learned that Pearl Harbor had been attacked. My dad just said, "Now I know why the planes were there." Shortly thereafter war was declared all around.

I truly believe that my dad's interest in and knowledge of the world affairs made me Think.

"Pat, there are more important things in this world, than one's own personal concerns. I quickly pulled myself together and realized that my "problems" paled in comparison to what was happening around me.

I focused on making all new friends and would you believe that one lives here in Payson, today? She is Joan Nadeau Hardway. We met when we were nine or ten. We talk on the phone almost every day and get together when we are able.

Notably, it was a very sad and lonely Christmas that year. My brothers and their friends were talking about joining the service.

I can't even imagine how hard it was for the parents of young men of "draft age" to even comprehend their decision to join the service. My poor parents!

New Year's Eve came and went with very little fanfare – no one knew what lay ahead.

CHAPTER 3
1942 - AND BEYOND

My sister, Merle, married Joe. Both Ben and Joe were assigned to the same Coast Guard cutter and were sent, in the dead of winter, to the North Atlantic. Horrific duty. I remember seeing pictures of ice laden ships. Something I have never forgotten.

Rents were scarce and it was never a surprise to see someone sleeping on the couch. "Don't ask!" was the phrase.

David was accepted into the army and was sent to officer's candidate school in Ft. Belvoir,

Virginia. He became a member of the Army Corp of Engineers. Mom, Dad and I went to his graduation. I cannot remember when he went to Europe, but it was soon after graduation, to join the fighting forces.

Nel, was turned down, because of his height. (I think it was one inch off.) He tried so hard to be accepted. He argued that his talents, highly technical repairs etc., required "sitting." <u>NO</u> <u>DICE</u>! I believe that not being able to be directly involved in the war effort, had a profound effect on him.

Ann's brother, Howard (I knew him as "Bud") was sent to the China, Burma, India area right near "The Hump." He repaired the new B29's and what a job!

My dad, volunteer that he was, joined the Auxiliary Police, in Connecticut. He was a longtime member of the N.R.A. (National Rifle Association) and had taught gun handling, maintenance, and safety for years. I learned, at an early age, about guns.

My mom discouraged my learning to shoot. I have always regretted that. He also worked in other capacities, but they were never discussed.

This is the year that the word Volunteer became a part of my vocabulary. Little did I know that this would play such a huge part in my life.

The elderly lady next door to us loved to play cards (not quite my cup of tea.) Every week we would play "Go Fish" or some other simple game and that made her happy. I also sat with a beautiful older woman, wheelchair bound, when her daughters needed me. She was always smiling. She was such a delight. When she died, I cried my eyes out.

Then, I got my first paying job- twenty-five cents an hour - "children sitting" for a house nearby. One time the people had a group of neighbor's kids in – "Oh, boy," I said. "More money!"

Twenty-five cents an hour – I guess it was more <u>volunteer</u> than a JOB!

I do not recall much more about 1942. We were all preoccupied with World War II and the safety of friends and relatives overseas. I wrote letters and helped as much as I could.

I kept very busy. My homework had to be finished before I could go out and play softball. Of course, I had piano practice daily. How I hated those scales. Very grateful, later on.

I wanted to learn how to cook, especially the wonderful desserts my mom made. "No," was the answer. "Too many people in the kitchen already." This is my excuse for my "microwave" gourmet meals today. When I was married, I had full time help – "such is life, Cest la vie."

In school we had frequent practices in case of a bomb attack. (Totally worthless in my opinion.) One night I had a dream about an attack. I will never forget it. It was down-right frightening.

I was happy in my new school. I loved my teacher, Joseph Foran. Later, he became very well known. He told me that my dad had talked to him early on, about the importance of EDUCATION, and he never forgot it.

Great news – Merle and Joe were going to have a baby. The year ended happily in that respect.

In 1943, we were all looking forward to the new baby, which was due sometime in the summer. In those days you could not determine the sex of the baby ahead of time.

Then, we learned that Joe's mother had died and left two young children. Teddy was eleven and Joy was ten. It was so sad that his mom didn't live to see her grandchild. Merle moved to Rochester to be with the children.

Both my parents, now in their fifties, said, "The children can come live with us." Remember their remark, "We take them (children) as they come." I was delighted. I felt as if I were now going to have siblings of my own age – Joy is seven months older than myself. I still kid her about that.

It is hazy in my mind when they came to live with us. I think a year or so later?

That summer, my mom and I went to Rochester, New York, to be with Merle. Joy and Teddy were there. The three of us had a "fun time" swimming in Lake Ontario and going out to dinner. When I say, "fun time," I am in no way diminishing the grief that Teddy and Joy felt for their mother.

At the age of ten, I became an aunt. Merle and Joe had a baby girl, Christy Lee. She was the most beautiful little thing that I had ever seen. (Probably not as pretty as I was, but we kept her!)

Mom and I returned to Woodmont and mom tried to keep the house in order. Just about impossible at the time. She still loved her baking, and she would say, "My hobby and my relaxation time."

Her culinary expertise had already been discovered. Once again, people were dropping by "just to say hello," and sample her tomato soup cake, her lemon meringue pie, her famous chocolate cake, etc. I can tell a "box" cake, every time.

My dad was, still, a big reader and kept up with the events of the day, especially political. I know that he and my mom were worried about David, Ben and Joe, but they kept their feelings private.

Dad was always knocking out a wall in the house or adding a room. This was "<u>his</u> hobby and relaxation time." He was a self-taught electrical engineer and many other things. He could build a house from the "bottom up." He and my brothers brought wood down from Maine and built us a beautiful cabin in Southbury, Connecticut. This particular wood was special, but I never knew why.

He helped design one of the first night baseball parks in the world.

He worked for General Electric, at the time. I believe it was in West Haven. Connecticut. He was always inventing things, but never got patents for them. Interesting man.

My mom loved her walks. When I was very young, we walked every day. She would point out the plants, the birds, the flowers. That is where I found my love of nature. We walked every night, weather permitting.

By the end of 1943, we learned that Rena was pregnant. Her baby was due in June or July. I, once again, was thrilled.

Joy and Teddy were with Merle, and I was jealous (kidding), but they were able to be with Christy.

CHAPTER 4
1944-1946 - TO THE END OF JUNIOR HIGH SCHOOL

*R*ena had moved to St. Augustine, Florida. I could never keep up with their schedules. Ben was stationed there, but he was out to sea.

Her baby was due in the summer, but she was not doing very well. My mom felt it best to take me out of school very early. It was essential to be with Rena.

I did have to make up the classes I missed, so arrangements were made. I did not mind at all.

When my mom saw my sister, she was furious. Rena was overweight and had edema. I think my mom was afraid she would lose the baby.

My mom got right to work, as she was no novice at having children. Somehow, she knew instinctively what to do. I think that she saved the baby and possibly my sister, too.

On June 12, 1944, Cheryl Lyn Meyer was born. We all said, "She looks like Ben, in diapers, and laughed. She was beautiful to us, anyway, and we <u>kept</u> her.

That summer we spent most of the time in St. Augustine. We even took a tour of the city in a horse drawn cart. We did go out to eat, often. One delicious beverage I still make is what they called "tropical Frosties." Today, we would call them "smoothies."

This was the first time we ever saw people bring "doggy bags" and take food home. Shocked US.

I often would go to the beach to watch the shrimp boats come in.

Shrimp was very inexpensive then. It had not really caught on. I might be imaging this, but I recall seeing large ships (war) way out in the ocean.

St. Augustine was fascinating. There were so many things to see and do. The oldest house in Florida was on our street (St. Francis.) It was a busy city and I really enjoyed learning about it.

My dad was up north, working all hours and somehow fitting in his volunteer jobs. He was now a "plane spotter." He would receive a letter from David once in a while and pass the news (what the government allowed) on to us. Mom always kept a stiff upper lip. She kept most things to herself, and I would hear her crying softly many nights. I hate to think of it!

Rena and baby Cheryl moved to Flagler Beach, Florida. Ben, now, was doing land duty – my sister would sit alone night after night. (No lights were permitted.) Ben patrolled the beach as German saboteurs were known to be coming in by submarine and various other means. Many were caught. Rena told me what a terrifying experience it was at that time.

The war was still in progress on June 6, 1944–when D-Day, the invasion of France, took place. We found out later that David had gone into Utah Beach on the second wave. We did know that he had been in London because he was dating an English gal. Finally, on May 8, 1945, the war in Europe came to an end. There were many celebrations all over the world when V-E Day was proclaimed. It was a great day for our family because David would be coming home soon! Joe and Ben were safe and well- Halleluiah!

~ ~ ~

In the fall of 1944, I went back to Central Grammar School in Milford (after the two-year hiatus.) I had forgotten most of the "GOOD" friends that I missed so badly, "back when!" They had forgotten me also. Funny, how things that often affect us so much at the time, just disappear or are no longer important – in our future.

I now was in the seventh grade and had one year after this until I would be in high school. Both years I kept very busy. I was taking ballet and told "I had a great deal of promise." I continued with piano lessons and that proved to be very worthwhile. I did a great deal of writing (mostly poetry.) Here is a poem I wrote entitled *Ghosts of the Theatre*.

GHOSTS OF THE THEATRE

When everyone has left the theatre
After the show is through
And nothing remains but a memory
And a forgotten dancing shoe.
Then the ghosts of "has been" actors play
Before five thousand strong
And Vaudeville is back once more
With dances, jokes, and songs

In theatre life one day you're known,
The next you're gone from sight.
Another "has been" actor
Playing with the ghosts at night.

~ ~ ~

I also wrote the words to my
class song, "Our Dear Old School." I
still have the original written copy.

OUR DEAR OLD SCHOOL
C.G.S. is a grand old school with
colors gold and blue.
She's a brightly shining symbol to
which many hearts are true.
C stills stands for Courage which
will carry through the years.
G is for the Guidance that has led
us through our fears.
S is for Sincerity of purpose taught
us here
By beloved teachers whomever we
hold dear.
We thank you for the hours here,
both sad and happy too
And in a lowered voice we say, we
hate to be leaving you.

C.G.S. is grand old school of colors
gold and blue.
And in a lowered voice we say, we
hate to be leaving,
Hate to be leaving, hate to be
leaving, you!

By Pat Hurlbut

~ ~ ~

When I was rummaging through
an old trunk in the attic, I found
several beautiful costumes my
sisters had worn, when they
performed. I found out that, none
other than my dad had designed
them and made them.

I also found a boxing glove and
discovered that my dad had been a
very good athlete and had done
some boxing, in his day. I did not
take up boxing, but I decided to take
up sewing. I loved it.

When I showed my mom some of
the outfits I made for my dolls, her
comment was, "Looks like
something I do." I knew that she

was not being negative, on purpose, so I was not discouraged. Then I got a "C" on a skirt I made in "Home Economics." End of that career.

There was one habit that I wanted to BREAK – I was constantly late. It seemed like most of the exercise I did, was running after the school bus in the morning. My mom said to me, "Patti, START TEN MINUTES EARLIER." Those words stick with me today. Now, I am usually early!

I never liked to read, as I was a slow reader. I took a speed-reading course, but I was told, "You probably have dyslexia. Today, I am never without a book. The problem now is that I hate to put it down!

I must say that both my parents had excellent educations, albeit just high school. I took one of their tests one day that they showed me. I was blown away. My mom was always first in her class, but unfortunately left school early because of her worsening eyesight. She went to some of the best specialists in New

York City and they could not help her. Her migraines were so severe; she would have to retire to a dark room (which would seem like hours.) However, her memory was phenomenal, right up until the day she died.

My dad continued to keep up with world affairs and would help me, at times, with my homework. Before I could go out and play soft ball with "the gang," I had to have homework completed, piano practiced and sometimes dishes washed. <u>Discipline</u>.

My parents were great. I could have friends over – We would often go to Savin' Rock, in West Haven, for fun and frolic and the auto races. Also, we would go over to "Paul's" who had the best hamburgers in town. I never had pizza until I was in high school. My brothers always went to New Haven for the "best pizza." When they told me it was tomato pie, it sounded <u>awful</u> and declined.

When TV came along, mom and

dad loved to watch wrestling. Don't laugh. They became experts! When they weren't too busy with other activities, they watched "The Soaps." I even heard my mom ask my dad, "What color hair do you think "Baby Doe" will have? When I said, "Mom, this is a Soap!" We all laughed.

Friday night was "movie night" and we hardly ever missed going to Milford to the "Crook." My favorite actor and actress were Alan Ladd and Lana Turner. You still cannot beat the old movies, the costumes, and the innuendos, which went completely over our heads, at the time.

Sunday, of course was church. For me Mary Taylor Methodist Memorial. All my friends went to the Congregational Church; (no way for me, I was told. (Dear Grandpa.) I was told, "You are a Methodist."

As it turned out, I loved living in Woodmont. We had the beach, weather permitting; picnicking, biking—just plain fun. Not far from my house was a miniature golf course. My father had designed and carried out the lighting for playing at night. We had a Jai alai Stadium nearby. So many things to do!

The bus stop was right at our corner. It went one way to Milford, the other way to New Haven. I often went to New Haven to Malley's to buy clothes.

I haven't thought of this incident in a long time. One day, I was waiting for the bus. A car pulled up and a man from the passenger's side got out. He was very well dressed and looked like a golfer. He came towards me and said, "Come on we'll give you a ride." My neighbor, Mrs. Malone, was looking out the window of her home and as she did, she hollered to me, "Patti, are you alright? With that, the man dashed back to the car, and they sped away. Mr. Malone, her husband, was a policeman, and it got back to my family. It was a rare occurrence, then – so prevalent today.

My dad had a good job at Bullard's in Bridgeport and when he had a vacation we usually went north. He loved New Hampshire and Maine. We had a favorite spot in Hanover, Maine and we had to cross over on a one car ferry to get to our destination (around Bethel, I think.)

One time we stopped to see friends. I thought that their "outhouse" was quaint- my mom told me later that some people in northern states did not have indoor plumbing. I was shocked and found out later, it was true.

When we went out to dinner, mom and I always looked at the desserts first. I found out that now my daughter Shari, does the same thing.

How I loved those trips. I was the navigator. In the back or in the front of my mind was always the desire to see the world! It is still numero uno on my <u>Vision List</u>.

Those years went by quickly. At the end of the school year, after graduation, I went with a date. to a school dance I became smitten (not with my date.) No worries, I will name the person who caught my attention, in the next chapter.

CHAPTER 5
HIGH SCHOOL YEARS AND COLLEGE

*I*n the last chapter, I promised to tell you more about my first dance. I think I wore a dress of Merle's. It was borrowed anyway, but I felt like the "cat's meow" nevertheless.

The band played the music from my sibling's era and beyond, which I loved. I did not listen that closely. My focus was on the trumpet player. I learned, later, that his name was Lester Hawks. Mickey DiBiase was also in the band. I remember that night very well!

I had a few "crushes," they call them, on cute boys. Les was older, a Junior or Senior. I can't remember which. (Certainly not a boy.) I was thirteen. I never thought much about it, after that. The summer lay ahead.

For my dad's vacation, we went to New Hampshire to some of his favorite spots. We went to Conway, which we really liked, Bretton Woods, where the big Monetary conference was held, and over to Franconia Notch.

My dad decided to drive up Mount Washington. My mother was really afraid of heights. I became hysterical, because of her fear. I spent most of the time on the floor by the back seat. How my father kept his composure, I do not know.

~ ~ ~

That summer, the days passed in quick succession and before I knew it, I was in high school.

For some reason or other, the

first few months caused me much anxiety and angst. I guess just "teenage insecurity"? I was getting my footing, so to speak.

I asked myself the usual questions which most teenagers ask themselves - "Will I be able to keep up with my studies? Will I be popular? Am I attractive? What does the future hold?" To me it was a scary time, for a while.

In my class, there was a very pretty girl. Her name was Joan Hawks. Les Hawks was her brother. I don't know what I said to her, but Les called me and asked me out. I was flabbergasted, to say the least. We dated for a long time, and I have pictures of us at two proms. We parted as friends. I thought the world of him. (My first big romance!)

Les and I often double dated with my good friends, Ann Cornwall and Mickey DiBiase. They eventually married. Mickey was a great guy. Those days sure bring back so many memories.

I believe that this was the time

Joy and Teddy came to live with us. I finally had siblings my own age. Now we had a "Blended Family" and it worked out well. We had the usual chaos, as most families do, but we got over it quickly! We were too busy living.

Joy and I were in the same class in Milford High School. I believe Teddy was at private school, Williston in Massachusetts.

Joy and I double dated occasionally. Joy was Catholic and I really enjoyed going to church with her at St. Mary's in Milford. I liked the service in Latin. I didn't understand it, of course, but the rituals were impressive.

I kept up with my studies. I had an active social life. I always had a new, long gown to wear to every dance and my date <u>always</u> wore a tuxedo! That was the fashion.

A group of us got together and started our own sorority in high school. We felt like the existing sorority did not reflect our particular values. <u>Nothing against them</u>. I am still in touch with three of the members. Joan Klages Lowe- I've known Joan I believe since Kindergarten and Carol Brough Shank and Barbara Voorhees Abbott, both, since grammar school.

In recent years, I discovered Barbara was my ninth cousin. She was always one of my favorite people. It was a surprise and a delight to discover that we were related. Two (first and only) husbands are still alive as well. Sadly, Dick Shank has died. I recently sent a birthday card to Bill Abbott. I called Jack Lowe for his 90th birthday on November 16th, 2021. I hope to visit all of them this year. I am eager to drive across the country, to visit friends and relatives in different states. I've lost track of the number of times I have made this trip alone.

I would be very remiss if I did not mention our good friend, Sue Woodmansee, from Milford High School. I was talking to one of my friends the other day and we both agreed that Sue was our "Sex Advisor." I know that I was "dumb as a brick" in that department. I was dancing with a boy, one time, and one of my classmates asked me, "if he had a mouse in his pocket." It took me years to figure that one out.

A group of us would sit in awe at the knowledge that Sue had on the subject. We still laugh about it today.

Another wonderful friend of Joy's and mine was Audrey Earnest. I used to save her a seat on the bus, on the way to high school. This was, of course, after I stopped running after it.

Audrey married Joy's older brother, Bob. A happier marriage you couldn't find, despite the age difference. He helped my parents out financially, with his younger siblings. I loved him, as he always treated me like a sister. Bob was a special person and so was Audrey.

~ ~ ~

My mom continued to encourage me to keep up my piano lessons and of course my dancing. She sang in her church choir. Her lovely alto voice could be heard clearly.

One night when we were out walking, I asked her what stimulated her to have such a profound interest in the theatre and music, etc. Her reply was a total surprise.

Her grandfather, McLean, on her mom's side and his wife, Mary Dubois, were prominent in New York Society. They had a box at the New York City Opera House and their friends were well known.

Her grandfather opened a restaurant, which catered to the noted performers of the day. My mom became interested in show business. She added that the other side of the McLean family lived in Washington, D.C. and they also were very well known. Apparently, there was friction between the two sides.

She briefly mentioned a cousin,

Neddie, who would come over to see them from D.C. for a visit. He was around her age, and she liked him. Her father, the Reverend, did not approve of her interests. Her brother, Harry, went to Yale and wanted to major in "Drama." Her father put a damper on that quickly. Her brother, Wilbur, a graduate of "dad's" university, Wesleyan, went into the Methodist Book Concern – that was just <u>FINE</u>.

Sometime after this, I saw an article about an Evalyn Walsh McLean who owned the Hope Diamond. It turned out that my mom's cousin, "Neddie" was Edward B. McLean, whose dad ran the Washington Post at the time. Evelyn Walsh's father struck it rich in the gold market and she and Neddie were husband and wife.

I never did find out what the rift was about. I suspect it was political or it could have been that Neddie married an Irish Catholic – a big thing at that time.

My mom's sister, Isabel was a

supervisor at the New York City Phone Company and in later years, she would see Neddie. He would come to ask her for money. She witnessed his continuing decline from drink and his unhealthy lifestyle. He was finally placed in a secure facility, unable to care for himself – so very sad!

~ ~ ~

I was nearing my graduation from Milford High School. Some of the girls were discussing their "hope chests" and talking about future marriage plans. `My hope lay in going to New York City to study dance and see if a career in Show Biz fit the bill. I really did not think about marriage, and I thought "maybe, someday!"

I graduated with honors, from Milford High School in June of 1950. Our class was the last and final class to graduate from that building.

I believe it became an assisted

living facility. The next high school was named after Joseph Foran, my sixth-grade teacher. They could not have picked a better man.

I rarely have <u>Regrets</u>, but this is a <u>huge</u> one. My ballet teacher, Jack Quinn, arranged an audition for me with George Ballanchine, choreographer and co-founder of the New York City Ballet. I was sick that day - NERVES. Jack never spoke to me again. I did not blame him. At 14 years of age, what a stupid dope. It totally freaked me out.

Travel was "numero uno" still on my VISION List. I wanted to visit every state in the U.S.A. I wanted to visit other countries and learn about their cultures. I wanted to attend a performance in Moscow of the Bolshoi, go to Vienna to enjoy its music and attend a performance at the Vienna Opera House, go to the Louvre in Paris, the Uffizi Galleries in Florence, etc. I wanted to spend some time in Egypt, which had been the true catalyst for all this interest in <u>TRAVEL</u>. Israel interested me, because of my religious beliefs.

College for now was my parent's choice. I had a chance to go to Wellesley. My mom's cousins were childless, and they wanted me to stay with them and go there, I felt it was still too much money even with the generous offer, so I opted to go to Storrs, Connecticut, to the University of Connecticut. When I saw the University of Connecticut for the first time, I thought it was the end of the earth! I saw a lovely church and a few structures, but little else – nothing like it is today. I moaned – "No one will ever find me here!"

My academic record for two years was a dismal failure. I met one man there that I really liked – Charlie Edson. The reason I mention him now is there is an anchor I see on TV often by the name of Edson – (maybe he is his grandson?) Wouldn't that be a small world?

One special person I must mention is Eddie Mentzer. I met him in Maine one summer. I went to see him at Brown a few times. In later years, I had the humbling task of having to tell him his father had passed away. We were meeting in New York City. I did ask for God's help. Many years later I was attending a conference at Brandeis University, and I called him. He was still happily married, and it made my heart sing!

~ ~ ~

Now off to New York City, and interesting adventures I had there!

CHAPTER 6
NEW YORK

I finally went to live in New York City. I moved into the Parnassus Club, a women's facility, not far from Columbia University. Shortly after I moved there, we had a party and students from various colleges were invited.

I sat next to a man, (I will call him Sam.) He was studying for his master's degree in business administration at Columbia. He was graduating in the spring and then going into the Air Force. We began talking and it felt as though we had known each other for years. From that night on, we spent as much time together as we could. I was taking ballet lessons at Ballet Arts on 56th Street. I did do some modelling and I had a job at a local night club. Sam was dedicated to his studies.

Shortly after Christmas, some friends came into town, and we all went to the village for dinner. Sam had an exam, and he did not go. He always knew his priorities. I was disappointed.

Two gentlemen, in naval uniforms, came in. One man, named Melvin Ward, was taken with my roommate, Annie. The other man's name was Bill Sellars. They were staying overnight in the city. Annie, a fabulous cook, invited them over for dinner the next day.

Melvin invited Annie to a party in Washington, D.C. where they were stationed. Annie was reluctant. Bill, in a very off handed manner said, "Pat why don't you come along also?" We went.

I continued to date Sam. I

thought, "perhaps this is the man I will marry someday." I loved him very much and he returned my love "tenfold."

In the spring I attended his graduation at Columbia. Averill Harriman was the keynote speaker. I promptly fell asleep. I had a late night, working at a club. I was exhausted. Sam was very gracious, and he understood. His mother was not pleased. She was not happy with his choice (me.) His dad and I got along famously. His mom had made plans for after the ceremony. Sam told her, "No, Pat and I have already made plans."

When we were alone, he said to me, "Pat, my parents have paid for my education. I am very appreciative. Now, I am finished and under no obligation to them, I will make my own living.

I did not doubt for a minute that Sam would be successful at anything he chose to do.

My parents had just told me, "Come home and go back to college, or we will cut off funds." I immediately got a better job and it felt great to be on <u>my</u> own.

The months with Sam were some of the happiest in my life. He told me, the happiest in his, as well. We were soul mates and compatible in so many ways.

At this point, however, neither of us knew what lay ahead. He was leaving soon for Scotland and the Air Force.

Just before he left, we had a long talk. Neither one of us were in a position to make a commitment. Circumstances, simply, were not favorable to our relationship, at that time. We would be more than two thousand miles apart and both trying to figure out what we wanted in life. We parted, friends. It was the saddest night in my life. He left me with a love letter, which I kept.

I found out recently that Sam had died several years ago. He married and had two children and a very successful career. I am sure that the woman he chose knew she was loved very much.

It broke my heart when I learned he died after a long illness.

~ ~ ~

New York City was an exciting place to live. Up until recently, it was still my favorite city in the world. <u>Now</u> <u>it</u> <u>is</u> <u>a</u> <u>disgrace</u>. So very sad!

I had plenty of jobs, in night clubs, in the city and other states, as well. They paid very good money. One of the jobs I had, I think in Philadelphia, the money stopped. This is when I found out about other jobs with <u>excellent</u> remuneration.

Another dancer and I were told to go to see a lawyer about the non-payment and he would help us with our problem. We found the lawyer's office and we were escorted into a huge room which was very elegant and upscale.

The lawyer, behind the desk, told us that we didn't have to worry about not getting a paycheck. With that, two very good looking, well-dressed men, came in and sat down.

By the time my savvy friend, with me, got finished telling the lawyer what he could do with the money, one of the men left in embarrassment.

That was the first of many offers I had, to be a High Class "call girl!"

One owner of a club said, "Bob, his wealthy customer, wanted to put me up in a very expensive apartment in the city. I really had to think fast, and I told him that I appreciated the offer, but I was "a kept woman already," but not to say a word to anyone. He apologized profusely.

I had a job in a club quite a distance from where I lived and the owner and his driver used to drive us back to the city every night.

One night one of the head waiters I knew, John, said, "Pat tell the girls not to accept any more rides." I commented that I especially liked the driver and that he was always so pleasant. John said, "he is a bodyguard and a very dangerous man. The Feds are after both men and so is the mob." I quit after that!

One very memorable ride I had, with another gal Jean, was one for the "record book." She and I had made some very verbal comments about certain things in the business, that we didn't like.

There was a gentleman who frequented the particular club where we worked. We got to know him. One evening, he asked Jean and me if we would like a ride back to Manhattan. He had to go into the city on business.

I believe the ride lasted well over an hour. It was pitch black and all we saw were the outlines of the trees, no houses, or lights and a very desolate countryside. The man, behind the wheel kept up a very casual conversation and then dropped us OFF at a bus stop.

We got the message and kept our mouths shut after that. We never saw the "gentleman" again- At least we got out of the car alive!

To supplement my income, I did some modelling. I remember one job well. It was for a weight loss product. They dressed me up with extra padding. Then I changed into a leotard and looked quite "shapely." The ad assured the viewers that after taking the product for several weeks, here was the result! (Several minutes was more like it.) Then the photographer asked me if I would like to go over to Forest Hills for the weekend. The big tennis tournament was on. I assured him that I had already been invited and I would look for him there. (Ha ha.)

I also found out that "strippers" were paid very well, at <u>certain</u> <u>places</u> in town! I could go on and on forever. Don't get me wrong. I have always felt that a person has the right to choose any job they want. I have always been (in my way of thinking) more secular than clerical and I am not being critical. Particular jobs <u>are</u> <u>just</u> <u>not</u> my cup of tea, (so to speak.)

I met some <u>very</u> <u>nice</u> <u>people</u>, and

I was asked to go out with some <u>well-known performers</u>. However, it was time to look elsewhere for other work.

I worked at Lord and Taylors for a while. I also worked in the office at Chase Manhattan Bank – <u>Big Regret</u>. I was offered a chance to learn the computer, and I turned it down. (Crazy girl.) It intimidated me!

~ ~ ~

Several of my friends from high school came to live in New York City: Barbara Hirtle and Sue Woodmansee. Barbara moved in with Annie and me. The three of us got along very well. We lived right off of Fifth Avenue, near Astis, a fun restaurant, which we frequented. It closed in 1999.

One weekend my cousin, Elmer Wilcox aka Junie, came for a visit. He was at the University of Connecticut when I was there, and he was like a brother to me. I asked Annie if she would mind being his date for the weekend as we had several dinner parties to attend. She said, "O.K." It wasn't that many months later when she and "Junie" were married. A happier marriage, I have not seen in a long time! They moved to Truckee, California and had a very successful business there. It was quite well known.

I loved Annie and I am so happy that she became part of our family. She was a bright and very talented woman. In later life, we travelled quite a bit together. They are both gone now, but I still miss them!

I roomed with Sue Woodmansee and she always kept me "on my toes." When I came home from work one night, Sue told me about the sexual antics of one of our neighbors, across the courtyard. I was totally baffled as our windows were so high, you could not peer out. I mentioned that. She had a big smile on her face and said simply, "Stand on that chair!" I laughed so hard at that one.

Sue married a fraternity brother

of Junie's – Charlie Brewer.

~ ~ ~

We went to many plays and at that time, *standing room only,* was ten dollars. When we could afford it, we would go to the New York Opera House to hear the famous singers. A "must" was tea at the Plaza and a trip to Trader Joe's, when the "purse" allowed.

Theatre was at its best during those years in the early Fifties – "South Pacific with Mary Martin and Enzio Pinza. I took my mom and she loved it, "The King and I" with Yul Brynner and so many, <u>many,</u> more.

I tried out for one up and coming play – "Wish You Were Here."

I made two cuts, but I had never had training in "jazz" and did not know the routines. Fun thing to do, however!

I was accepted into a French Company (name eludes me now,) but they did so much touring that I opted out.

New York City was a magical place to this nineteen-year-old. Some of my experiences certainly were "interesting adventures."

I met Bill Sellars there. (Need I say more?)

New York City had something for EVERYONE!

CHAPTER 7
MARRIAGE

I remained in New York City for a while. As I said, I had some good paying jobs, but I finally looked at the overall picture of my life. I was not meant for a career in "Show Biz." I certainly was not competitive enough. I did not share the same values of many of the people I met, either. Nothing against them!

At the same time, I began dating Bill Sellars. How our relationship evolved, I do not know. Our first encounter was "unspectacular" to say the least. Over a period of time, I found that I was falling in love with him. It was a different love than the one that Sam and I shared, but it was real. Bill had never met my parents. I went home, alone, to see them and to tell them about the new man in my life. I had a picture of Bill and I showed it to my mother.

My mom was very psychic, and she stared at the picture. She had an instinctive "feeling" about people which was uncanny. Her comment was, "Patti, this man will never make you happy, or give you the things you really need. He is very cold."

"Oh, mom," I said, "If, or when we get married, things will all work out." I remember the conversation well.

A few months later, Bill asked me to marry him. I accepted. We were married in New York City. His dad had given him a large sum of money, which I thought was very nice. However, it was none of my business and I forgot about it. I have made my views clear on money, previously.

Bill made a decision to leave the Navy, when his term was up. I was pleased because I was not cut out to be a serviceman's wife. I had seen enough of that with my sisters. We moved to Washington, D.C. for his final year.

Almost from the beginning, I had some serious, nagging suspicions about Bill's veracity and his fidelity. I chalked it up to my imagination and decided to ignore it again and again because "everyone loved Bill.

We moved to New Jersey, after returning north. His parents wanted us to move into their lovely home in Short Hills, New Jersey. They were never there. We opted to get a house of our own.

Believe it or not, we looked at nice little houses in Red Bank, New Jersey for $15,000. Bill did not like them. He and his dad found a house for twice as much in Springfield, New Jersey on Sharon Road. It was in the process of being built.

It was very nice, but when I spoke about money to finish it and furnish it, Bill said, "My dad said you spent enough already." I was <u>furious</u>! I thought, *who is running our life here?* I immediately went to his father. It turned out that his dad never made that statement. In fact, he said to me that if I needed money for myself, he would give me $450.00 monthly, and asked me if that was enough? He also said that the money he gave to Bill was for BOTH of us. I thanked him very much, but I declined his generous offer. I made it clear that I did not marry Bill for his money.

This incident made me really wonder about what kind of marriage I had gotten myself into. I was in love, just got married, and so tried to forget my feelings about the incident.

His dad along with several other people owned a large stevedoring company in New York City. Bill went to work there, on the docks.

Then the company was sold and his father at the age of 78 years old at the time, retired.

~ ~ ~

Bill and I decided to start a family. In 1957, we had our first daughter Shari Ann. In 1958, a year and a half later, Deborah Leigh was born.

Bill did not want me to work. I figured that I was home anyway. I might just as well have two tots to raise, at the same time. I loved being a mother, which surprised me! In 1962, Karen Lynn, appeared on the scene, planned, as the others were. A little while after Karen was born, we moved into a beautiful house on Cedric Road in Summit, New Jersey. The architect was Royal Barry Wills.

We had a myriad of friends. We entertained a great deal. Bill loved parties and going out to dinner. He did not like travelling (of course, my great passion,) but he liked to go on cruises, which we both enjoyed.

We took the children on vacations, and they had their own particular activities. We spent many summers in Sea Girt, New Jersey with his mom and dad. (Beautiful home. Seven Baltimore Blvd.)

It looked like Bill and I had everything, but that was not true. Our relationship was deteriorating. I could never have a discussion with Bill that he did not turn it around and blame me for something. I always ended up the "guilty party." I finally sought help. It became apparent that I was not the only woman in Bill's life.

One of the psychiatrists I went to for a while said to me, "I don't know how to fix your relationship – you've tried everything possible." By that time, I understood "why." So, I went to a lawyer for advice. Under New Jersey law, at the time, I might end up with nothing. It was his father's money. The children would be going back and forth between our homes. I imagined what that would be like for my children under the present circumstances. So, I made my choice (RIGHT OR WRONG) to stay, for the children's sake.

I told <u>no one</u>, not even my best friends. No one. I kept up the charade. It took its toll on me.

~ ~ ~

Our last move was to a 178-acre farm in Litchfield, Connecticut.

I hoped that somehow things would improve, if Bill were not so close to the city! But, HELL NO! <u>I</u> took a great deal of his abuse, but <u>never</u> physical abuse. Later on, I came to understand that emotional and mental abuse is often far more insidious.

I endured it because I felt my children were the most important part of my life. I wanted the best for them.

Bill's parents loved the girls and gave them everything. I truly loved his mom and dad – great in-laws! And I feel the love was returned.

I said to Bill one day, "Your mom and dad are so generous, but when each child reaches the age of sixteen, they will ask for a Mercedes." I was half kidding, but I wanted to teach my children that having things given to you, without working for them, was a very bad idea." I was pleased that they were hard workers. I still wanted to get that point across.

Before any one of you thinks that this is a fabrication, let me remind you that the truth "ain't" always pretty. I did not like being a "Trophy Wife," a misnomer, to begin with, in the first place. A "front" would be a more appropriate term. I still felt trapped.

I am not denying that I had many amenities – beautiful homes, full time help, all the money I needed and much more! However, people who think all this is compensation, have very limited values or morals.

I have to say, that in spite of it all, Bill was an excellent father. He loved his children. He and the children each had a horse. Bill had been an equestrian and I believe he taught horseback riding at the Hill School, a private school that he had attended. He spent many hours with them. The girls were in Pony Club and participated in many local events. Bill and I were both involved in the final Litchfield Horse Show. The girls loved animals and could have any animal of their choosing – but we drew the line at lions and tigers. Our stipulation, "Never let us hear you complain about caring for the animals, or we will give them away." Some of their menagerie included sheep, goats, gerbils, mice, rabbits, and Guinea Pigs.

Now I will add a quick story: Karen was griping about her horse Lockie. He was a stubborn cuss. Lockie wasn't performing and he wouldn't do her bidding, she complained. Our response was, "Well, we will get rid of him." (what BS that was.)

In the next few months, at an

Equestrian Event, no one recognized Lochinbar. (No, we didn't paint him a different color.) It was amazing the time and effort that Karen had spent training him. And it paid off because everyone wanted to borrow him after that event.

Karen had another horse later on, who apparently thought of himself as a dog. (His thought, "What, *me* jump that fence? You got to be kidding!" We gave him to Kent School where he transported the kids around. How diligently Karen had tried!

~ ~ ~

Bill tolerated most animals, but years before the children wanted a cat. Bill's retort was, "over my dead body." So...when we brought the cat home that night, the cat went immediately to jump on Bill's not so dead body. But that night, who was outside frantically looking for the missing cat. Need I say more?

I am adding a bit of levity here by telling you that when we moved to the farm, we were surprised to find that we inherited 33 cats with the farm! We had to spay and neuter many of them. Bill fed and watered them, which cost us a fortune!

One day Bill received a letter from a tenant. It was in the form of a poem which I include here:

I do not like my room at all.
The quarters are so
cramped and small.
I cannot stand the colors
here,
They're gray and brown and
lack all cheer.
It's drafty, dark and cold as
ice.
And not a roommate I find
nice.
The bed I guess is made of
hay
So narrow, I fell off one day.

And the neighbors on my
right

Keep me up with sex all
night.
That dog of yours, his name
is Scout.
He chases me when I go
out.
I know that I should not
complain,
And that I am a royal pain;
For after all, the rent is free.
Without your help, where
would I be?

With all this said, I love the
chow,
And I ain't leavin'.

Chief Meow.

~ ~ ~

We built our house quite a
distance from the barns. Bill bought
a snowmobile for transport during
the winter and a "Terra Tiger" for
the summertime use. Bill also
bought a small transport device to
transport things to haul behind the

snowmobile. Sometimes the kids would hop on the carrier and Bill would drive them across the long expanses of the fields. One day the kids hopped on the carrier, and a few minutes later, Bill hit a bump and the kids went flying off into the snow. They laughed their heads off. Bill was totally unaware and kept going and went way across the long field. When he turned around to look back at them, he was astounded. The expression on his face when he saw the empty carrier was priceless.

When the children wanted to raise Labradors, Bill helped build a whelping pen and assisted with the puppies' birth.

On one of the children's vacations, we went to New York City. When we left, we had a bitch ready to give birth, and when we returned, we found twelve puppies! At the time we had a German housekeeper, Nina. She was trying to explain to us that she had found a puppy outside in the snow. She had not understood us when we told her when we left, that the mother dog was not to go outside. Then she commented to us, "I brought it in and put it in the oven." We all gasped together. She then tentatively replied, with the gesture that told us we did not understand what she was trying to tell us. Then she picked the little puppy up and handed it to Bill.

"No, no, no! She explained, "Incubaby. Incubator!!" We all sighed with relief.

~ ~ ~

I had never been west and Bill was going to rent a Winnebago and we were going to travel across the United Utates to the west coast with the children. But when we told Shari and Deborah, they said in unison, "Oh! We can't do that!" Bill and I looked at them in amazement. It seems that the breeder we knew had a kennel and they were going to work there when she went on her vacation. It ended up that we made them promise that they would be available the following year. Bill and I both laughed and said, "Who are the parents here?"

Bill was wonderful to his own parents and then later when they became ill, he kept them at home with nurses around the clock and I felt that was money well spent and I was glad it was there to care for them. His mom after a while had a serious case of dementia. Later in my life, I worked with many people with dementia.

My mom and dad grew to love Bill. He was as good to my parents as he was to his own parents. When my dad and mom came north in the summer, they stayed with us. Bill went to all the children's games, made sure they had the best education, going to prep schools nearby and when it came time for them to attend college, he let them choose their college and I was proud of the children that they were never looking for a handout.

At this point, however, the charade of our idyllic marriage was wearing thin. I found out about one of his lady friends, Nancy C. She lived in a upscaled apartment on 65th St. in New York City. Then, one day, coincidently, his brokerage office called and asked me, "Should we send the papers Bill requested to your home or to your apartment. I replied, "We don't have an apartment in the city." Less than two minutes later, his secretary called back and was profusely apologetic because she had made a mistake." I had no interest anymore to follow it up for the truth. And I finally broke down and told my dearest friend, Barbara about my long-time situation. She found it hard to believe. I simply said, "I know this woman's phone number and I talked to her."

At this time, all of my girls were almost out of school. When I confronted Bill, he confessed that he did not know how many women he had slept with, but I was the ONLY one he ever loved and begged me to stay. I tried it for a while. We talked. I was aware that he had his own money and credit cards. We agreed on a settlement. It should have been a very simple procedure. After that, I went to a well-known lawyer. I saw him more often on television than in person and our divorce dragged on for another year and a half.

Someone asked me one day, how come you weren't in court last week for your divorce. I did not know a thing about it and had to change lawyers again and by that time, I just wanted it to be ended.

It dragged on more than was necessary for sure.

~ ~ ~

I do not know why Bill married me. I found out later that Bill had told many lies about me. However, the one that made me chuckle the most was, "I can't leave Pat because she could never take care of herself." Don't get me wrong I am FAR from perfect, but I never cheated, our marriage was sacred, and I oppose divorce. In retrospect, I feel that the problems with Bill started <u>long</u> before I came into the picture, and long after.

Even when he was planning to marry again, he was overheard bragging about the women he had been seeing during our marriage.

Go figure. Regrets I have none, as I made my choice and stuck with it. I have the satisfaction of knowing that I did everything in my power to fix it and more important, my children turned out well.

I have gone on to live what I consider a very productive and rewarding life.

CHAPTER 8
AGE

*W*hen I speak of age, I always think of age as just a number. I do not mean to be blasé. It is easy for me to say, as I do almost all of the activities I've always done, for years. I still drive, and I have planned a trip east, soon. I want to see friends and family, who are living in different states.

Aging has its consequences, good and bad! Some people, however, use it as an excuse and abuse it. I do not like phrases such as, "I'm not as young as I used to be, so therefore..." or "that it is due to one's age."

In my most recent move, I kept hearing, "Make sure your condominium is near a hospital." Or, "Make sure your condo is on the first floor; stairs are too dangerous."

Heck, I've been going up and downstairs since I was a "kid."

I never heard my parents refer to age, or illness, either. (Well, I am wrong.) I asked my mom one day, if she would like to visit friends in a nursing home.

"No," she said, I do not care particularly for old people."

My brother said, "Mom, you are over eighty years old."

"I know," she replied quickly, "but old people depress me."

After my father died, my mom at the age of eighty-four had a marriage proposal. It was a good offer and a true story.

She said to my sisters and me, "I am not marrying any old "gink" and taking care are of him." Our bridesmaid dresses had to go back.

Shortly, thereafter, she went into

the hospital for a routine procedure.
While my sisters and I visited her at
her room in the hospital, a nurse
came into the room, stopped short
and said, "Wrong room! We are
waiting for an OLD woman." We just
laughed.

At age 47, I had to think of age.
After my divorce, I asked myself,
"What job would always be available
to me, if I remained healthy?" My
answer was, "Care Giver." I can even
work today if I wanted to. I went
immediately to Oliver Wolcott
Technical High School in Torrington,
Connecticut for my C.N.A.- Certified
Nursing Assistant. I never aspired to
go into the health field, but I loved
it!

In 1990 I completed my college
degree at the University of
Connecticut, with honors, while I
worked nights as a C.N.A.

I had started in 1950 at the
University and quit, after two years
to go to New York – remember?

Recently, I came across a
congratulatory letter from the head

of the department of Extended and Continuing Education.

In part it read: "I nearly burst my buttons at the listing of B.G.S. grads... over two hundred and fifty of you!" It went on to say, "I sense that the degree means more to you, as a returning adult learner, than it can possibly mean to your younger classmates. I sincerely wish you success in the future. We are proud that you selected the University of Connecticut and the Bachelor of General Studies Degree and even prouder that we can count you among our growing number of B.G.S. alumni. Congratulations and best wishes. Sincerely, Dee Herschel, Ph.D., Dean."

Folks, it only took me forty years! You are never, ever too old. I graduated at the age of fifty-seven.

I took a course at the University of Connecticut on Women and Relationships. I was reading a chapter on emotional abuse. Then it hit me like a bolt of lightning. Emotional abuse is so subtle, and the abuser is a master manipulator. No one is the wiser. It fit my marriage to a tee. Bill knew how to keep his double life and make himself look like the victim. What a relief it was to me to finally understand that at last.

Immediately after graduating from University of Connecticut, I was now looking for a Master's Degree in Native American Studies. My daughter Shari had moved to Tucson, so I decided to take a leisurely ride across the country. I stopped at several universities. I found the program at the University of Arizona best fit my needs and I applied. It took only a limited number of students, and I was turned down.

I wrote back immediately and questioned them – "Was it my age?"

"No," they responded. "Please apply again."

Instead, I had the opportunity to take a hospice course at the Sunrise Chapel in Tucson. That is where I learned about Reiki. I had always been interested in healing. It was on my "VISION List." I then moved to Tucson, and I decided to take a refresher course for my C.N.A. certification in Arizona.

One of the first lessons concerned sex and the older person. I presumed it was for the younger nurses. Maybe not?

The instructor was very good. She worked at an Assisted Living Facility. Recently, two people there, had "tied the knot." Both were in their late eighties. She could not find a queen bed for them, so she put two twin beds together and left for the night. In the middle of their "tryst," the beds came apart and the "newlyweds" fell onto the floor. NO injuries, but our instructor was called.

The young nurse on duty that night, was furious and told the instructor to, "Come at once!" The instructor listened to her story and couldn't help laughing and went back to work.

By this time, I was laughing too

since no one was hurt. She did exactly what I knew she would. First, determined whether there were any serious injuries. When assured none, she put the beds back together (more securely,) bid the lovers a pleasant "GOOD NIGHT!" and left!

The moral? SEX has no age limit! Just remember, kids," "Knock first, before opening the door!"

Over the years I worked with so many different situations, I found that a sense of humor often got me through it when all I wanted to do is "give up and cry."

I worked as a C.N.A. for over thirty years. I, also, worked as many years, or more, as a hospice volunteer and several years as a paid worker. I became a Reiki practitioner and was in one of the first groups to practice Reiki in the Tucson hospitals.

I lived in Green Valley, Arizona for many years. Five of those years, I volunteered at the Animal League of Green Valley. I then started my own dog walking and dog sitting program.

~ ~ ~

Recently, my sister Joy's stepson, Alan, brought her over from Texas for a visit. It was such a "joy," in more ways than one. She is living with Alan and his lovely wife, Hope, and you can see the love there.

We chatted about many things and what I didn't remember, Joy did. It must have been so difficult for her to have her life turned upside down, at such an early age.

Joy has been very successful despite her many bouts with cancer. I never heard her once complain when I called to talk with her. I love her dearly, but wish we were closer and could do things together. At least she is not too far away. I can drive over to Texas once in a while.

~ ~ ~

People look at aging in so many different ways.

When I was young, I would hear men and women, in their forties, gripe about their aches and pains and how restricted they were. I would see others in their seventies, eighties and even in their nineties out skiing, playing tennis, and enjoying every minute of their lives. I'd think to myself, "What's wrong here?" So far, I have succeeded in enjoying my Golden Years. I am looking forward to many more!

I wrote two poems on aging. Here they are:

ON AGING
Strike a balance between work and play.
Allow yourself freedom of expression.
Laugh at yourself.
Be more loving to the person who is you.
Do not let ego-driven thoughts destroy you.
Make room for the soul, your

witness:

Let it be involved in quiet reflection.

This is the time for better understanding of "Self."

Enjoy your wrinkles, you earned them honestly.

They are a sign of laughter and mirth,

A sign of sadness and grief, and

A life well lived.

The second poem is:

LIVE IN THE MOMENT
Cease to dwell on the memories

Of the past, they are not real.

Waste not a minute on the future,

It does not exist.

Live only in the mystery of the moment,

And....... that is all there is.

Lastly, Eat more chocolate and less veggies.

Aging as I said, can be both bad and good. Many times, it is the way you approach it – illness as well.

I believe if more people would look at things in a more positive manner, an ATTITUDE SHIFT would make a visible difference all around.

CHAPTER 9
ATTITUDE SHIFT

Change is swift, "but not always as swift as one would like it.

I spoke to an 82-year-old friend, who is recovering from three operations in the past several months. I asked him, "What part, if any, did attitude play in your recovery?"

"EVERYTHING," was his immediate reply.

My nephew, Gary, in his seventies, is facing some cancer challenges. I call him often and he always makes me laugh. The other day, the nurse asked him, "What finger can I use for your blood draw?"

"Yours!" was his reply. He has always had a sense of humor.

To me, laughter is the consummate healer, and we sure need more of it today!

LAUGHTER
Laughter is the consummate healer,
the one we can count on
when we are down.
Laughter's hand on our shoulder
urges us to let go,
to be free and to happy.

When I started working with hospice, I was invited to a lecture given by Doctor Bernie Siegel, a noted cancer specialist at Yale. I was very reluctant to go – (thinking all I would hear is sadness and heartache.)

I did go and it changed my entire attitude about cancer. Dr. Siegel emphasized how important laughter was or is. In another lecture, in Las Vegas, his speech gave even more meaning to the work I did with death and dying. To me, helping people make the transition is profound and very deep.

Big ATTITUDE SHIFT, for me.

My Aunt Mabel, who I mentioned earlier, had breast cancer. For eleven years, she was fine. It came back with a vengeance. She lost weight rapidly and was down to sixty-four pounds. The doctors were amazed that she was still living.

I went to see her. She had a big smile on her face She wanted to know all about how I was. Never once did she allude to her condition or the cancer.

Two days later, she called my dad and wanted to see him. She asked him to make sure "her Cliff" would be cared for. My dad assured her that Cliff would come and live with them.

That night, my Aunt Mable died peacefully, in her sleep. She always thought of others <u>first</u>.

Uncle Cliff went to live with my parents, and he was a joy to have around. We loved him. He died several years later.

My nephew, Gary, fits right in here.

To me, a POSITIVE ATTITUDE is "GOLD."

Another example is my Uncle Bill. When he was in his eighties, he had a leg amputated, due to diabetes. He waited patiently, for a prothesis. Finally, he asked the nurse about it. "Oh, no" she said. We do not do that at your age."

He said, "well, you had better make an exception." They did and he got around much better than people half his age.

When I saw people, who seem to have everything, it used to make me wonder why are they so unhappy? Granted, some people like to be that way, (for personal reasons.) We all know a few, or more, of those, don't we?

Over a period of years, as a C.N.A., I've observed the behavior of so many people, sick, well, old, young. Now for me, it is not hard to figure out why. <u>We do not walk in their shoes.</u> However, we all have the potential, <u>within ourselves</u>, to change our lives if we want.

I can hear the "nay sayers," "They say, "Now, Pat, you have no idea!" I say, "Oh, yes, I do!"

It became harder and harder for me to keep my secret. I began to think it was my fault that our marriage was failing. Even the counselors had some doubt.

There was a time in my life, when I thought it was hopeless and I thought of suicide.

From the outside, it looked like I had it all. I had money, beautiful homes, three lovely children and a <u>WONDERFUL</u> husband, etc. etc. The unhappiness - I kept it to myself. I drank. I knew, intellectually, it was stupid, but that was my "coping mechanism" - (I am not very proud of it.)

One day a wise counselor said, "Pat, you will still be in this situation at ninety. You cannot fix it. <u>IT TAKES TWO!</u>

I got up, looked at her and said, "THANK YOU. NO MORE!" The truth finally came out! A surprise to many people and counselors alike.

I got a divorce and I never looked back. I had some marriage proposals, (very <u>good</u> offers) but I declined.

Now even in dire circumstances, I look for a different approach.

ATTITUDE SHIFT (not so swift) but a <u>BIG ONE</u> in my life. My key to <u>FREEDOM</u>.

I am sure that there are many, many people, who want to make changes. It takes "beaucoup" discipline, and it is not easy. It sometimes takes a long time I know.

For many years, I have taken time to pause, periodically, and reflect upon my life. What changes do I deem necessary, (like old habits no longer relevant)? What future goals do I want to see and how am I doing overall?

My brother, David, told me that

he did the same thing.

When I speak of changes, I am not referring to material acquisitions or making more money. I mean concrete changes, which enhance your life, add balance and equality, and make you a better, happier, and more productive person." I do not dwell on it! I say to myself, "Knock it off – you are blessed. You are grateful. You are thankful and you are fortunate." Then I pray for those who are <u>really</u> suffering.

I take that minute to pause and make a mental note:

I have a lovely condominium.

I have all the material possessions I need – (I hate a lot of stuff!). I am a minimalist. I do not have a great deal of money, but it is a fun challenge to work within my <u>BUDGET</u>.

My children and their families are all successful -and generous.

What I want most, is to remain independent as long as I am able.

Right now, I am concentrating on having this book finished -and published.

In the <u>FUTURE</u>, go back to volunteer work, which I love. Go back to fun activities and spiritual activities that add so much to my life; and go back to <u>WORK</u>.

Until recently I walked 4-7 dogs, six days a week. I am a dog walker and a dog sitter.

When I see people with severe difficulties having a good time and living life to the fullest, it makes my heart sing.

How many people <u>could and should</u> be out there, enjoying life, if only they would make an ATTITUDE SHIFT (and find the GOLD.?)

How about you?

CHAPTER 10
STAYING FOREVER YOUNG

*W*hen I started writing this book, I said that I was writing it partly to look back on my life and that even with my years of experiences I might possibly learn something in the process.

Did I ever!

My life has been quite a journey. Certainly, no overnight success or failure. It has taken perseverance and discipline. Discipline is a must, but just about impossible without FLEXIBILITY. So much has happened in my eighty-eight years on this planet.

My adventure has taken me far and wide. One lesson I learned quickly in layman's language, so to speak, when you are thrown from the horse, get up, dust off and get back on the horse.

Move On. Life is not always a smooth ride.

As a child and just beginning to write, I wondered why there were no books written to tell you how to live and deal with what lay ahead.

I was young and naïve, and I wrote my own Mission Statement. I have tried to follow these four simple rules, throughout my life:

1. To learn through education and intellectual pursuits.

2. To live by the principles and values handed down to me from my parents.

3. To get out of myself and help others. When I see a "need," spontaneously fill it.

4. To take care of myself, emotionally, physically, and mentally in order to be a viable person.

Obviously, I have deviated from the course, occasionally. I have always thought that GOALS are necessary. I started my VISION LIST when I was in the first grade, as you know, travel was number one and remains "numero uno" to the present day.

Volunteering has played an important part in the scheme of things. Someone asked me one day "Why are you so involved in many projects?" I facetiously said, "When I hear the word 'volunteer', my hand automatically goes into the air."

Here is a partial list of volunteer jobs that I enjoyed doing that added greatly to my own life. Feel free to become involved in anything that reaches your heart:

Hospice, Homeless, Habitat for Humanity, Child Welfare, Audubon, Junior League, Church Work, Nursing Homes, Meals on Wheels, Stephen Ministry, Counseling, Battered Women, Senior Centers, Animal Shelters, American Association of University Women,

Reiki, Trail Maintenance, Hospitals, Brownie Leader, Girl Scout Leaders, Political Centers, Teacher Assistance, Native American. Reservations, Global Volunteers, Work, Construction crews.

Seriously, I come from a long line of ministers and missionaries. Jonathan Edwards, a well-known minister in the 1700's was also a scholar and a philosopher. He graduated from Yale University in the early 1700's. One of the first residential colleges at Yale bears his name. Somehow, we are related (possibly he is a grandfather?)

I have had the privilege of travelling all over the world. For about twelve years, I combined travel with my volunteer work.

I've worked in Africa, South America, Nepal, Mexico, and other various places in and around the United States. I certainly have done many diverse types of jobs.

When I look back at the things that I have participated in, I am proud. I've also had my own businesses. I feel that all these activities kept me focused and sane, during the difficult years of my life.

One of the biggest revelations came when I realized that being a volunteer is not just helping others. It is two-fold. It is a very important mechanism for one's own personal growth, through both teaching and learning.

My most important years, as a volunteer, were the ones I spent caring for members of my family.

Merle died in her seventies, and I went to Florida to help care for her. I was with her, in hospice, the morning she died.

Gary, the nephew I speak of in the book, is her son. Now seventy-five years young, (born in 1947.) He is doing very well.

My brother Nel became ill, and I went to live in South Carolina for a while. I brought him back to Arizona to live with me until he died at the age of eighty-eight.

Sister Rena was diagnosed with liver cancer (never had a drink in her life.) Ben was ill, also. I would go back on occasion to Connecticut to be with them. She died twenty days after Nel and unfortunately, I could not be there.

At the same time, my dear friend Barbara terKuile was sick. To this day, I regret not being there to help her in her time of need.

David survived World War II and went on to fight in Korea. He married and had two children, Stacy Erickson, who lives in Colchester, Connecticut and David, Junior who lives close to his sister. My brother had a very successful life.

I kept my apartment in New Hampshire and lived with him for about a year in Colchester. I was there when he died in hospice at the age of 92, on Memorial Day weekend. His combined funeral service - Veteran and Masonic was beautiful.

~ ~ ~

Of all the volunteer jobs which

affected me most, was working with patients who had dementia.

When one thinks of dementia, Alzheimer's disease immediately comes to mind. In 1906 Doctor Alois Alzheimer discovered cell damage in the brain of one of his patients, after an autopsy. Dr. Alzheimer was a well-known psychiatrist and neurologist, and the disease was named after him.

I have been told that today, with the new techniques, about 90% of the cases can be diagnosed without surgery. There are many types of dementia.

It became very personal for me – my father had Parkinson's Disease, which eventually affected his memory. He always knew my mom! Bill's mother started losing her way at the age of sixty and she lived for another ten years. The nurse and I would sit with her for hours and she never said a word. When Bill would come home from work, and she saw him, her spirits would lift, and she would have a beautiful smile on her face.

Dementia is an insidious disease – one of my patients did everything in her power to ward it off. The person is aware of the changes taking place from the very beginning. This lady hired people to walk with her every day and to keep her mentally stimulated.

It was heartbreaking to watch her decline.

I was conversing with another patient one day. Her sister was observing us from across the room. Later, she came over to me and told me she could never understand a word her sister said. I assured her that I was unable to understand a word she said, either.

I explained that my approach was to treat every patient with respect and dignity. When I was speaking to the patient, I acted as if I understood every word and that it was a perfectly normal conversation.

Remember, my first introduction to the disease was when I was seven. Every morning, when auntie

Irene would tell her stories over and over, I treated her with total respect and listened attentively. At the time, I didn't have a clue about dementia.

I wrote the following poem, which was inspired by observing many dementia patients in my care. It is my perception of what it may be like to be in their mind.

I'm Traveling on a Bus Through Time

I'm traveling on a bus through
time"
And peer through frosted glass
Somehow I cannot understand
The images that pass.
I'm cold, I'm scared, I'm hungry
too,
And want to run away
But briefly for a moment, know,
There is no place to stay.
Strange faces fill the dreary
hours
As time floats gently by.
Sometimes, it fades so slowly,
Sometimes, it seems to fly.
I see my mother standing there,

Her arms are open wide.
I see a little girl of three,
Who runs to her to hide.
I smell my mother's sweet
perfume,
And I see her loving smile.
I hope that she is here with me
To stay a little while.
She disappears into the mist.
I strain my eyes to see,
And then there's only emptiness
And nothingness for me.
I see a woman full with child
And hear a baby cry.
I search my dim lit memories,
I know them, yes, but why?
Oh, memories they come and go
Like butterflies that light.
They briefly show their brilliant
garb
And then resume their flight.
Like swirling leaves on autumn's
breeze,
A kaleidoscopic blend
Of smells and color, shapes, and
sounds,
Confusing to no end.
I feel it is the life I led

With happiness and tears,
But no matter how I try
I can't recall the years.
I spy a woman bent with age
Time's ravages I see
Her face is lined, her eyes are
dull.
Oh, no! That can't be me.
I glimpse a ray of sunshine.
It warms me to the core.
I try to hold it in my hands
And then it is no more.
I'm travelling on a bus through
time
Where will this journey end?
I stare out at the road ahead
But can't see around the bend.
I'm travelling on a bus through
time
I want to run away
But in my heart I realize
It's here I have to stay.

CHAPTER 11
MY FINAL THOUGHTS

Over the years my VISION LIST has continued to grow. Some of my goals were met, some fell by the wayside.

Always near the top of the list was to write a book!

Writing this book has been very emotional and frustrating. At times, I was not totally committed to the task at hand. I was neglecting other important areas of my life. I was feeling overwhelmed and scattered.

I even questioned whether I should continue. I asked myself that question and received a resounding

<u>YES</u>!!

However, I realized that I would have to make a few simple changes before I could carry on efficiently. I had to prioritize, have more effective schedule, and be organized!

I still have to have a place for everything and know where it is.

Before I can even begin my day, the bed must be made, plants watered, and make sure that there are no dishes in the sink. I try, after every snack or meal, to wash the dishes immediately. I do not use the dishwasher.

Keep in mind my age and status as a single woman. (No one else is around to mess things up.)

This may sound ridiculous to you but believe me it helps me have much less stress, anxiety, anger, and impatience.

Now when I have a busy day ahead and I begin to get anxious, I calm myself down. I remind myself to do things little by little. Take one thing and one day at a time. Let the day unfold. Live in the now (not easy to do.) Sometimes, I meditate for five minutes to take a break.

What I have learned from writing this book is much more than I anticipated. I hope, in some small way, it will be beneficial to others who read it.

Nevertheless, nothing can take away the sheer pleasure and outright joy I derived from writing it and finally bringing it to fruition. Today, I am FINISHED writing it.

Thank God for my gift of health and the ability and desire to continue to LIVE LIFE TO THE FULLEST.

Now, I wonder what adventures await me?

ABOUT THE AUTHOR

Author Patricia Hurlbut Sellars graduated from the University of Connecticut as a returning student. She received a BGS from the Department of Extending and Continuing Education. She is a Reiki practitioner and was in one of the first volunteer groups to practice Reiki at Tucson hospital. She is also a Stephen Minister. Pat worked as a Certified Nursing Assistant for over thirty years and as a Hospice paid worker and volunteer for many years.

Her love for travel and learning has taken her all over the world. Equally important was her work as a volunteer. For twelve years she combined both work and travel in the United States and foreign countries.

Made in the USA
Monee, IL
29 July 2022